Captain Joe
Teaching Resources

by Emily Madill

Captain Joe Teaching Resources © 2011 Emily Madill

www.emilymadill.com

Library and Archives Canada Cataloguing in Publication
E. Madill

ISBN 978-0-9812579-5-2

Printed in the USA.

Other books by Emily Madill:

*The Captain Joe Collection ISBN 978-0-9812579-4-5

*Captain Joe to the Rescue ISBN 978-0-9812579-0-7

*Captain Joe Saves the Day ISBN 978-0-9812579-1-4

*Captain Joe's Gift ISBN 978-0-9812579-2-1

*Captain Joe's Choice ISBN 978-0-9812579-3-8

TABLE OF CONTENTS

About the books:

The Captain Joe Series was designed as a tool for adults to teach children about constructive imagination. The four books are a fun and interactive way to introduce the concept of "Thoughts Turn Into Things" (so choose the ones that make you happy) to young children, ages five to nine years.

Joe and his thought-zapping superpower will invite children to use their imaginations to constructively choose thoughts that promote healthy self-esteem and self-awareness. Each story is designed to teach a key concept.

Children will be captivated by Joe and his encounter with Wilfred the friendly wizard. Wilfred presents Joe with a special wand that helps him take charge of his thoughts by ZAPPING away his unhappy thoughts and replacing them with ones that are happy.

The introductory story, **Captain Joe to the Rescue** is a great way to begin discussions with children around thoughts, attitudes and personal power in shaping them.

The second story, **Captain Joe Saves the Day** is a great way to open discussions around the importance of following our dreams in an appealing way kids will relate to.

The third story, **Captain Joe's Gift** is a great way to introduce discussions with children around standing up against bullying and celebrating our differences.

The fourth story, **Captain Joe's Choice** is a great introduction to discussions around the power of our thoughts and choices in creating our happiness.

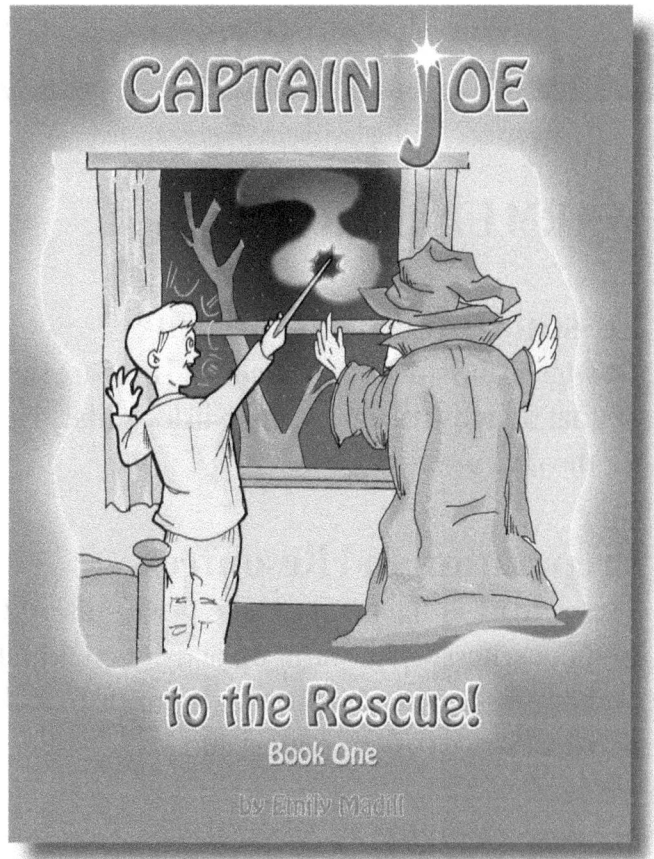

Using the books in the classroom:

The following six activities, based on the story **Captain Joe to the Rescue**, are intended for a Grade 1 - Grade 3 level of learners, specifically targeting grade 2.

Some of the activities may have to be adapted to suit the grade 1 level. As an example, in the Performing Arts Lesson, instead of separating the students into partners, the entire class could perform the activity together as one big group.

Handouts for the lessons can be found in the Activity Sheets Section. The Activity Sheets Section also contains a Story Sequence handout, Math handout, Word Search, and Spelling Vocabulary List.

There is also a "Comprehension, Word Study and Something to Think About" worksheet in the Activity Sheets section. The Something to Think About question could either be used as a journal writing activity, or the back of the handout could be used for students to write a longer answer.

Rubrics have been created for each of the 6 lessons as an assessment tool. These Rubrics could be adapted to suit the particular needs of your class. They could also be altered to assess a different learning outcome than the one stated.

Activity #1 - Performing Arts

WARM UP EXERCISE

Lesson Objective/Outcome
To engage the students mentally and prepare them to make pictures in their heads (visualize) of what their own magic wands will look like. This activity will also help prepare the learners for the next activity.

Preparation and Resources
This activity is intended to take place "after" **Captain Joe to the Rescue** has been read to the learners. The warm up activity could take place with students sitting comfortably at their desks with their heads down, or in a clear space where each student has enough personal space to feel comfortable.

See Page 19 in Activity Sheets Section for an easier to read Teacher Copy of the Warm up Exercise.

Lesson Idea
<u>HOOK:</u> Read **Captain Joe to the Rescue**

Let the children know that just like Joe they each have their own superpower and will be taking part in a class activity to "discover" what their own invisible thought-zapper wands look and feel like.

Organize students so they are in a safe, comfortable and quiet environment. Have the students close their eyes and lead them through the following exercise:

Close your eyes and imagine you are lying very still in bed just like Joe was in the story. Keep you eyes closed and now imagine that Wilfred the friendly wizard has just showed up at your house to give you your own magic wand. Think about how happy and excited you feel to get to see what your thought-zapping wand will look like. With your eyes kept closed still, imagine Wilfred is handing you your invisible thought-zapper wand, only it isn't invisible to you. You can see it. Keeping your thoughts to yourself for just right now...What does your wand look like? What colour is it? Is your wand very heavy or is it as light as a feather? Does your wand make noises or is it as quiet as a teeny tiny mouse? Keep your eyes closed, and now imagine you are holding your wand in your hands and you have the power to make it invisible to everyone but you. But, before you make your wand invisible, try to remember how it looks and feels right now at this very moment. Now that you know what your wand looks like, imagine Wilfred says to go ahead and make your wand invisible because it will always be with you whenever you need it. If you ever forget what it looks like Wilfred says to just close your eyes and imagine. Okay, very slowly you may open your eyes now.

Closure

A/B Partner Talk, children verbally describe what their wands look like to one another and then share one thing about their partner's wand with the class. Class discussion about the kinds of thoughts their wands can be used for, i.e. stopping the everyday thoughts that become self-limiting beliefs – e.g. "I won't bother trying because I won't be good it anyway".

A great follow up activity is the Draw & Describe Activity (see next activity) where students draw their wand and write three things that make it special.

Assessment

Please See Activity Sheets Section for Rubric

Activity #2 - Language Arts & Art Project

DRAW AND DESCRIBE

Lesson Objective/Outcome

To create a visual representation of the thought-zapping wand (key concept in this story), after the story has been read in order to confirm meaning and reflect on the story. Learners will create an image using one or more art element and in their sharing will demonstrate respect for their own work and the work of their fellow learners.

Preparation and Resources

This lesson is intended to take place after **Captain Joe to the Rescue** has been read and the learners have had the opportunity to take part in the warm up activity. Building this foundation will provide students with enough ideas to draw their own thought-zapping wands.

See Page 20 & 21 in Activity Sheets Section for the handout.

Lesson Idea

Students will each receive a handout with a space for drawing their wand, in colour, and a place to write down three things that make each of their wands special.

Display finished handouts on the bulletin board around the title, **The Amazing Grade 2 Captains.**

Closure

Students will take part in a class share with plenty of applause to boost their confidence. This could be done in pairs or individually.

Adaptation

There is a modified handout in the Activity Sheets section that gives assistance in the written description part of the lesson.

Assessment:

Please See Activity Sheets Section for Rubric.

Activity #3 - Drama Activity, Performing Arts

FEELINGS BECOME OUR ACTIONS

Lesson Objective/Outcome

For students to become aware that our feelings show up in how we look and act and these actions tell others something about us (e.g. he is happy). Students will also work on developing their ability to work co-operatively with others both in an observer role and in an acting role.

Preparation and Resources

This activity requires a clear, safe place, ideal for the gymnasium. The activity is intended to take place after the class has heard the story, **Captain Joe to the Rescue.**

See Page 22 in Activity Sheets Section for the handout

HOOK: Thoughts Become our Feelings
          Feelings Become our Actions
          Did you know our Actions tell the World Who We are

The hook concept is the basis for this activity and can be found on page 19 of **Captain Joe to the Rescue.** Students will have the opportunity to work in pairs. One student will read a card with a feeling on it, e.g. happy, sad, mad, scared and will then display (using a physical non-verbal action) what the feeling looks like to their partner. Their partner, in turn will have an opportunity to guess what the feeling was. The students take turns being the actor and the observer.

IDEA

Before you begin, read cards together as a class to make sure students understand what the feeling is and ensure they are able to read each of the words.

Lesson Idea

Students are positioned in a circle facing inwards. The teacher puts the students in pairs within the circle.

The teacher gives each of the students in the pairs a card with 4 feeling words on it - each of the cards will have different words (even if describing similar feelings e.g. mad may be on one card and angry on the other).

The teacher instructs the students to make up a physical non-verbal action that represents each of the words on the card.

The activity starts when Student A starts doing one of the actions, demonstrating it to the other partner, Student B.

Student B then has an opportunity to guess what the word and feeling was.

Student A will continue on with the next three words and after Student B has observed and guessed what all 4 feelings were, the partners switch roles.

Closure

Each pair of students will show the class their favorite feeling word to act out and will then let the class know what it was (option, pairs ask classmates to guess what they thought it was)

Extension

Display the verse below somewhere visible in the classroom to be utilized whenever a teachable moment should arise.

IDEA

> Thoughts Become our Feelings
> Feelings Become our Actions
> Did you know our Actions tell the World Who we are

Assessment

Please See Activity Sheets Section for Rubric.

Activity #4 - Language Arts

BRAINSTORMING, MIND MAPPING SESSION

Lesson Objective/Outcome
To help learners develop more awareness of the many different thoughts we have and how these thoughts can contribute to how we feel. To provide students with a tool to help self-regulate their moods and behaviours.

Preparation and Resources
Page 23 & 24 from **Captain Joe to the Rescue** is the hook and basis for this lesson.

See Page 23 & 24 in Activity Sheets Section for student handout & teacher reference of what the finished product looks like.

Lesson Idea
Read **Captain Joe to the Rescue** to class. Write the passage from page 9 on the board or overhead:

> We all have an amazing and powerful brain.
> We use it for making thoughts.
> Our thoughts come in all shapes and sizes.
> Some come from inside ourselves.
> Others happen because of things going on around us.

Each student receives a handout with cloud in the center for brainstorming ideas.

IDEA   Start the lesson out as a class, brainstorm various ideas of the different kinds of thoughts they have "ON A DAILY BASIS" to get learners started.

Note: there is a teacher copy of this handout for your reference.

Students can then finish adding different thoughts they have to their brainstorming bubble individually or in pairs. If time allows, students can add colour to their mindmaps.

Closure

Class share the various thoughts created in brainstorming session. Add a few of the answers to the Word Wall. A great follow up activity is Activity #5.

Create a space/poster in the room called "Thoughts Turn Into Things". Over time, add different thoughts to help students create more awareness around the different kinds of thoughts we have and how they make us feel.

Another idea, is to group thoughts. One Heading might be "Thoughts that make us feel Happy" or "Thoughts I Zap away with my thought-zapping wand".

Having the thoughts posted as a daily reminder could act as a useful tool in guiding children to better self-regulate their moods and behaviours.

Assessment

Please See Activity Sheets Section for Rubric.

Activity #5 - Language Arts, Art

MY FAVORITE THOUGHT PICTURE AND DESCRIPTION

Lesson Objective/Outcome
To begin developing conscious awareness and control of everyday thoughts and how they make us feel.

Preparation and Resources
Students will have already heard and will be familiar with the story, **Captain Joe to the Rescue.**

This activity is most beneficial after students have had the opportunity to think about what their own thought-zapping wands might be like and also after participating in the brainstorming session in Activity #4.

See Page 25 in Activity Sheets Section for the handout.

Lesson Idea
Students will pick either: 1) Their favorite thought they have from their brainstorming session 2) A thought that makes them feel really happy 3) A thought they have that they want to remind themselves to ZAP

Students will draw a picture of their thought, and write one sentence describing what the thought is.

Closure
Students will have an opportunity to share their finished products with their classmates. Drawings could also be displayed somewhere in the room.

Assessment
Please See Activity Sheets Section for Rubric.

Activity #6 - Art Project, Language Arts, Art

ART POSTER

Lesson Objective/Outcome

To create an image in response to the story, **Captain Joe to the Rescue**, and be willing to share and display the finished product. To work on good listening skills (while others are sharing) and good speaking skills (while sharing). If using Option #2, learners will demonstrate a willingness to work co-operatively.

Preparation and Resources

The book, **Captain Joe to the Rescue** for reference, Poster Board, Pencils, Crayons/Pencil Crayons/Paint.

Lesson Idea

Art Poster: Draw a poster that will advertise the story **Captain Joe to the Rescue**. Make sure to include the title of the book and the author's name. Write down three reasons why you think others should read this story.

Option #1: Students take turns presenting their completed Art Posters to the class

Option #2: Students work on this activity as a group in order to develop their ability to work co-operatively as a group. Each member of the group could take on a role: Time Keeper, Presenter, Summarizer, Recorder, and Cheerleader/Encourager.

Closure

Give opportunity for students to share and explain their completed Art Poster to one another. Generate class discussion about what kinds of stories students enjoy hearing or reading (intended to create enthusiasm around books and reading).

Adaptation/Extension

Students can work in pairs or in groups. Have students write a letter or email to Emily Madill, describing why they think others should read this story (Emily Madill will send out a response to student/class).

Assessment

Please See Activity Sheets Section for Rubric.

ACTIVITY SHEETS FOR
CAPTAIN JOE TO THE RESCUE

Captain
Joe to
the
Rescue

Captain: _____
Your Name

Comprehension :

1) Joe said all of his _____ make him feel dizzy sometimes, like his head is spinning around and around.

2) Who came to visit Joe after he had a scary dream?

3) What is Joe's wand supposed to be used for?

Word Study:

Please write these words in alphabetical order:

many	zap	wand	use	around

Add the suffixes "s" and "ing" to the end of these words:

a) walk   b) feel   c) pull   d) turn   e) tell

Something to think about:

Why do you think Captain Joe's wand is invisible to everyone but him?

Activity #1, Warm up Exercise

- Close your eyes and imagine you are lying very still in bed just like Joe was in the story.

- Keep your eyes closed and now imagine that Wilfred the friendly wizard has just showed up at your house to give you your own magic wand.

- Think about how happy and excited you feel to get to see what your thought-zapping wand will look like.

- With your eyes kept closed still, imagine Wilfred is handing you your invisible thought-zapper wand, only it isn't invisible to you. You can see it.

- Keeping your thoughts to yourself for just right now...What does your wand look like?

- What colour is it?

- Is your wand very heavy or is it as light as a feather?

- Does your wand make noises or is it as quiet as a teeny tiny mouse?

- Keep your eyes closed still, and now imagine you are holding your wand in your hands and you have the power to make it invisible to everyone but you.

- But, before you make your wand invisible, try to remember how it looks and feels right now at this very moment.

- Now that you know what your wand looks like, imagine Wilfred says to go ahead and make your wand invisible because it will always be with you whenever you need it.

- If you ever forget what it looks like Wilfred says to just close your eyes and imagine.

- Okay, very slowly you may open your eyes now.

Captain _____'s Thought-zapping Wand
(Your Name Here)

Write down three things that are special about
your wand.

1) _____

2) _____

3) _____

www.emilymadill.com

Captain _____'s Thought-zapping Wand
(Your Name Here)

Write down three things that are special about your wand. (Adapted Version)

1) Colour_____

2) Shape_____

3) Size_____

Card for Partner A

HAPPY

SAD

EXCITED

ANGRY

Card for Partner B

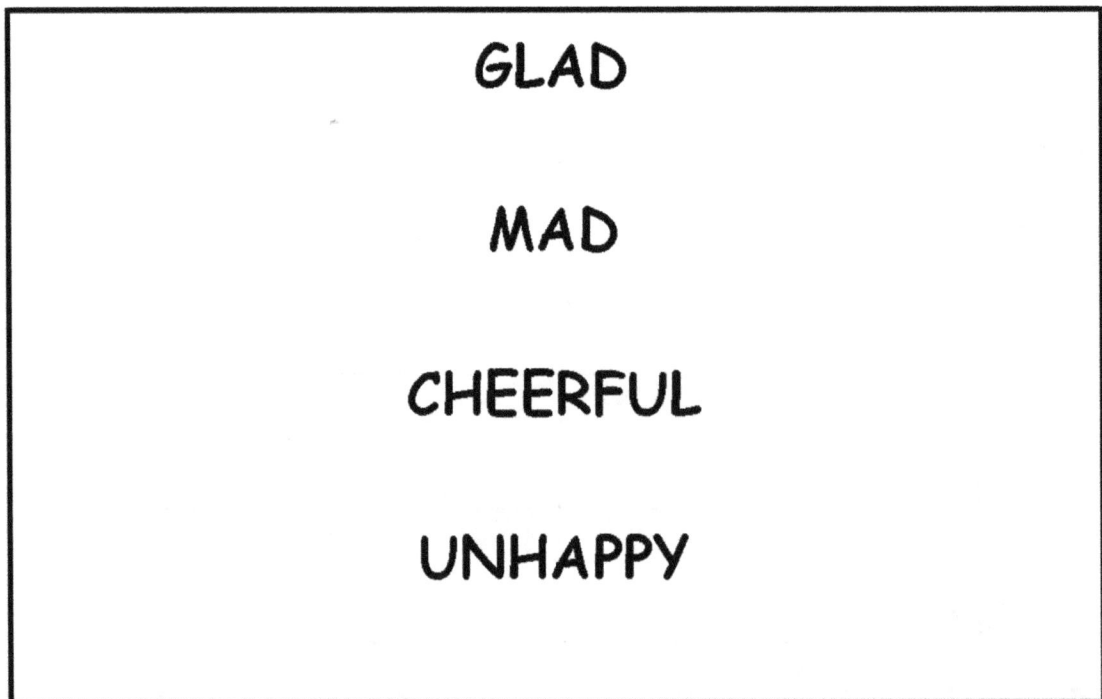

GLAD

MAD

CHEERFUL

UNHAPPY

Let's Brainstorm

Let's Brainstorm

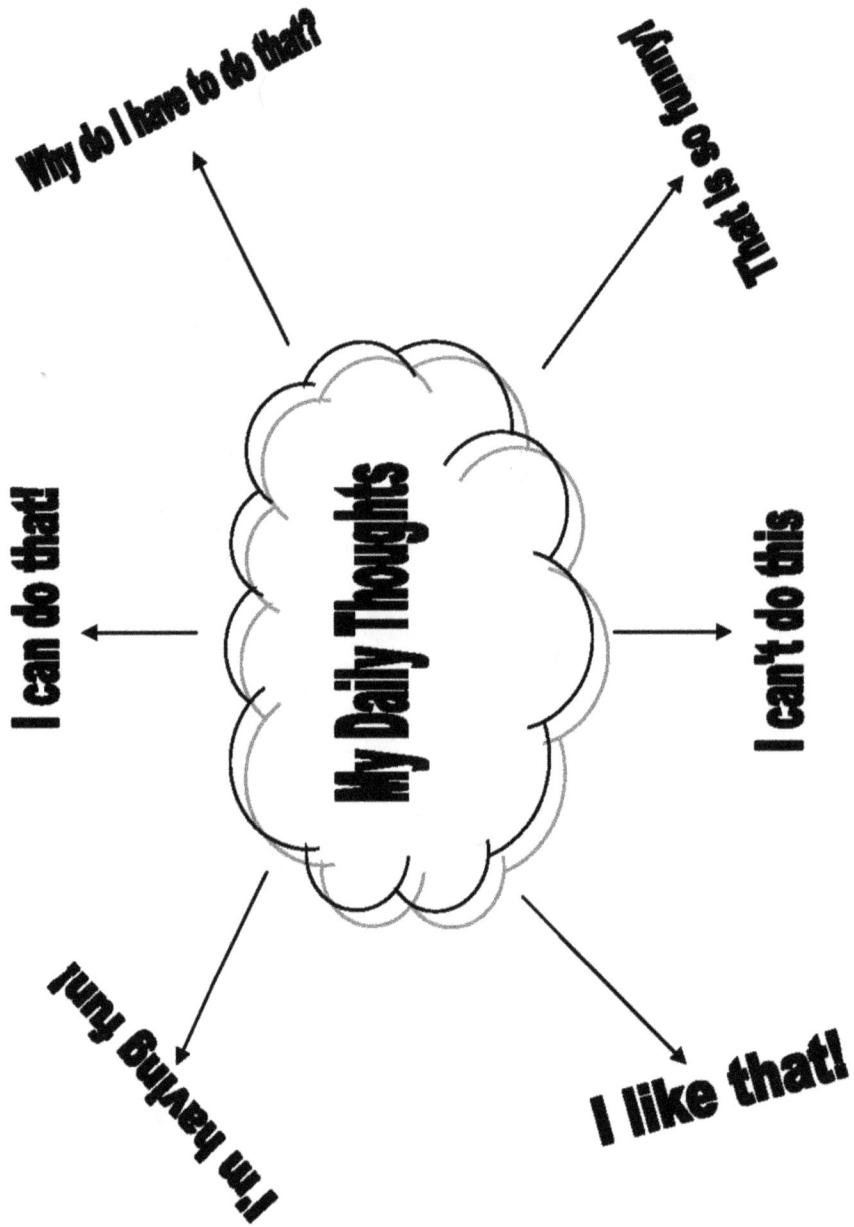

Why do I have to do that?

This is so funny!

I can do that!

My Daily Thoughts

I can't do this

I'm having fun!

I like that!

Captain: _____

(Your name)

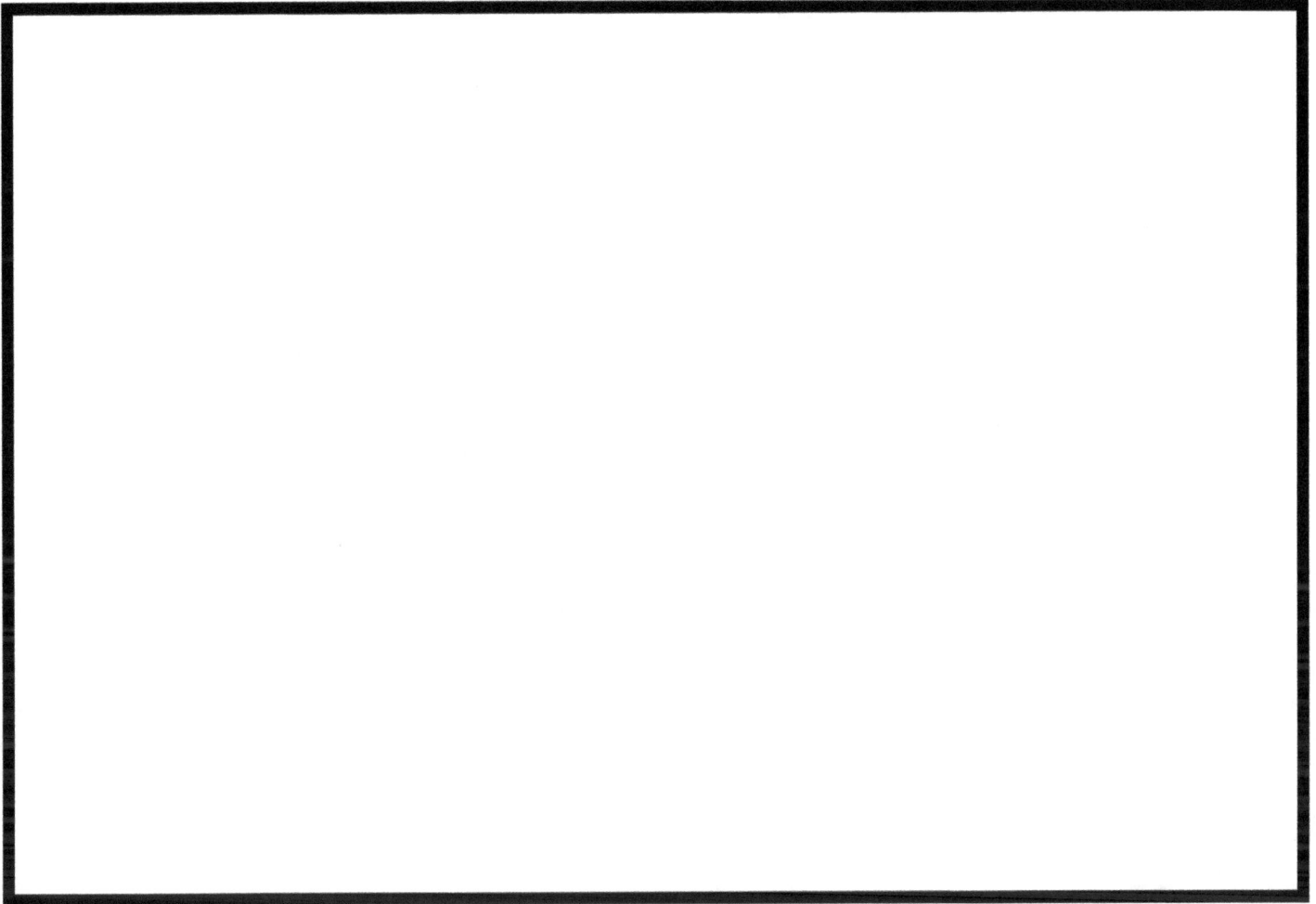

Vocabulary for spelling tests

always	power
boss	use
call	wand
Joe	Wilfred
pit	zap

* Please note: The above words are intended to be used, one or two at a time, as an addition to weekly spelling tests or as an addition to the Word Wall. The words range in difficulty level from moderate to more complicated.

Captain Joe to the Rescue Word Search

```
F K H O N X N R Y K R N B G T
P B W H E A I E W D K J Z W M
R T W V T O A W I K Q L L N L
C A L L W E T O L S Y A W L A
T K B A N O P P F O H U O D M
L X N G E J A S R O E Q R Z K
Y D C P A Y C U E Y A D A Y E
J L K S H G S Z D U S E G I X
I N Y B H Q O N G B X Y U A H
E B S G O O Q G J Y I E E R T
W R O C D K I J Y K C V D D C
S I J T L M P O K M K P I T J
Z S C K I E R U A F W A N I D
Y Y O C A P Z D W X C Z T O N
L G P B E M M C Z D Q O H Q D
```

Look for Words: frontward, backward & diagnal

ALWAYS	CAPTAIN	POWER	WAND
BOSS	JOE	TREE	WILFRED
CALL	PIT	USE	ZAP

Captain Joe to the Rescue Story Sequence

Beginning	Middle	End

In the Beginning: In the Middle: In the End:

Captain Joe to the Rescue Story Sequence (Adapted Version)

Beginning	Middle	End

In the Beginning:	In the Middle:	In the End:

<u>**Add**</u> the numbers in each box to discover what the message below says.

A   5
    7
  + 1
-------------- 	
	D 8
	    3
	  + 3
	-------------- 	
		G 5
		    3
		  + 1
		-------------- 	
			H 9
			    3
			  + 3
			-------------- 	

I   9
    5
  + 2
-------------- 	
	N 5
	    3
	  + 2
	-------------- 	
		O 1
		    2
		  + 3
		-------------- 	
			P 4
			    2
			  + 5
			-------------- 	

T   1
    2
  + 1
-------------- 	
	U 7
	    3
	  + 2
	-------------- 	
		W 7
		    8
		  + 2
		-------------- 	
			Z 10
			    5
			  + 3
			-------------- 	

____ ____ ____ ____ ____ ____ ____
 4   15   6   12   9   15   4

____ ____ ____ ____ ____ ____ ____
 18   13   11   11   16   10   9

____ ____ ____ ____ !
 17   13   10   14

Add the numbers in each box to discover what the message below says.

A 5 7 + 1 --------------- **13**	**D** 8 3 + 3 --------------- **14**	**G** 5 3 + 1 --------------- **9**	**H** 9 3 + 3 --------------- **15**
I 9 5 + 2 --------------- **16**	**N** 5 3 + 2 --------------- **10**	**O** 1 2 + 3 --------------- **6**	**P** 4 2 + 5 --------------- **11**
T 1 2 + 1 --------------- **4**	**U** 7 3 + 2 --------------- **12**	**W** 7 8 + 2 --------------- **17**	**Z** 10 5 + 3 --------------- **18**

T H O U G H T

Z A P P I N G

W A N D!

Assessment Rubrics

Assessment, Lesson 1

Outcome	Criteria				Total
	1 (Not yet)	2 (Meets)	3 (Fully Meets)	4 (Exceeds)	
Demonstrate good listening skills during teacher reading of "Warm up Exercise"	Did not listen or stay on task at all during the warm up exercise	Listened for some of the warm up exercise, but not all	Listened without speaking for the entire warm up exercise	Listened, kept eyes closed and appeared relaxed for the entire reading of the warm up exercise	
Demonstrate good listening skills during A/B Partner Talk	Unwilling to participate in A/B Partner talk	Willing to take turns listening, but interrupted or spoke out of turn	Listened without speaking while partner shared	Listened without speaking while partner shared and also paraphrased something back to partner that he/she said	
Demonstrate good reporting out skills during class share	Did not remember anything about partner's wand or was unwilling to participate in class share	Remembered one thing about partner's wand, but did not speak clearly or make eye contact with the audience	Remembered one thing about partner's wand, spoke clearly and made eye contact with the audience	Remembered one thing about partner's wand, spoke clearly, made eye contact with the audience and asked if anyone had any questions	

Assessment, Lesson 2

Outcome	Criteria				Total
	1 (Not yet)	2 (Meets)	3 (Fully Meets)	4 (Exceeds)	
Create Visual Representation of their own thought-zapping wand	Left Box blank or incomplete	Drew a picture of their wand, but did not add colour	Drew a picture of their wand and added colour	Drew a picture of their wand, added colour and added one more art element (e.g. pasted something on, painted etc.)	
Write three things that are special about their thought-zapping wand	Did not write anything about their wand	Wrote 1 or 2 things about their wand	Wrote three things down about their wand	Wrote three things down about their wand that were original	

Assessment, Lesson 3

Outcome	Criteria				Total
	1 (Not yet)	2 (Meets)	3 (Fully Meets)	4 (Exceeds)	
Willing to express themselves in acting out 4 feelings to their partner	Was unwilling to act out 4 feelings from the cards to their partner	Made an effort to act out 2 or more of the feelings from the cards to their partner	Made an effort to act out all of the feelings from the cards to their partner	Made an effort to act out all of the feelings from the cards to their partner and partner was able to guess what each of the feelings expressed were.	
Work cooperatively with partner	Was unwilling to participate in activity with partner	Took turns and stayed on task some of the time	Took turns, listening & acting and also stayed on task	Took turns, listening & acting, stayed on task and gave praise to one another for their efforts	

Assessment, Lesson 4

Outcome	Criteria				Total
	1 (Not yet)	2 (Meets)	3 (Fully Meets)	4 (Exceeds)	
Create a mindmap with 5 different thoughts	Did not brainstorm any thoughts for mindmap	Had 2 or more thoughts written down on mindmap	Had at least 5 thoughts written down on minmap	Had 5 or more thoughts written down on mindmap and added colour	
Work cooperatively with partner	Was unwilling to work with partner or share ideas	Worked cooperatively and stayed on task some of the time, shared some ideas	Worked cooperatively, was willing to share ideas and stayed on task	Worked cooperatively, was willing to share ideas, stayed on task, and gave praise to each other for either ideas or finished mindmap	

Assessment, Lesson 5

Outcome	Criteria				Total
	1 (Not yet)	2 (Meets)	3 (Fully Meets)	4 (Exceeds)	
Completed Drawing/representation of favorite thought and one sentence describing what it is	Did not draw a picture of favorite thought or write a sentence describing it.	Either drew a picture of favorite thought and did not write a description, or did write a one sentence description of favorite thought and did not draw a picture	Drew a picture of favorite thought and wrote one sentence describing what it was	Drew a picture of favorite thought, wrote one or more sentence describing what it was and added colour to the picture	

Assessment, Lesson 6

Outcome	Criteria				Total
	1 (Not yet)	2 (Meets)	3 (Fully Meets)	4 (Exceeds)	
Create Poster Board, including the title, author's name & 3 reasons why others should read the story	Poster included only 1 of the requirements stated in the outcome/directions	Poster included title & author's name and at least 1 reason why others should read the story	Poster included title & author's name and 3 reasons why others should read the story	Poster included title & author's name and more than 3 reasons why others should read the story	
Demonstrated good speaking/presenting skills	Was unwilling to participate in presenting poster	Willing to participate in presenting, could have spoke clearer and did not make eye contact with the audience	Willing to participate in presenting, spoke clearly and made eye contact.	Willing to participate in presenting, spoke clearly, made eye contact and asked the audience if anyone had questions.	

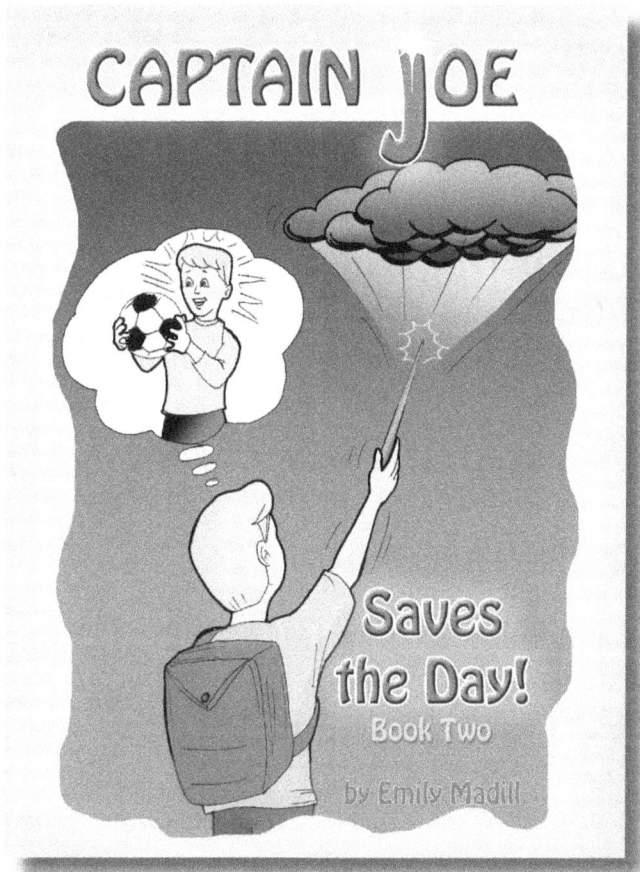

Using the books in the classroom:

The following six activities, based on the story **Captain Joe Saves the Day**, are intended for a Grade 1 - Grade 3 level of learners, specifically targeting grade 2. Some of the activities may have to be adapted to suit the grade 1 level. As an example, in the Performing Arts Lesson, instead of separating the students into groups of 4, the entire class could perform the tableaus together as one big group.

Handouts for the lessons can be found in the Activity Sheets Section. The Activity Sheets Section also contains a Story Sequence handout, Math handout, Word Search, and Spelling Vocabulary List.

There is also a "Comprehension, Word Study and Something to Think About" worksheet in the Activity Sheets section. The Something to Think About question could either be used as a journal writing activity, or the back of the handout could be used for students to write a longer answer.

Rubrics have been created for each of the 6 lessons as an assessment tool. These Rubrics could be adapted to suit the particular needs of your class. They could also be altered to assess a different learning outcome than the one stated.

Activity #1 - Language Arts

SWAMPY THOUGHTS VS. HAPPY THOUGHTS T-CHART

Lesson Objective/Outcome

To create a list of thoughts and classify these thoughts into 2 separate categories. To begin developing conscious awareness of different types of thoughts we have.

Preparation and Resources

HOOK: KWL Chart, give students opportunity to reflect on what they know from the last book, make some predictions about this book and get them excited to hear the next story, **Captain Joe Saves the Day**.

Read **Captain Joe Saves the Day** to the Class

See Page 49 in Activity Sheets Section for the handout.

Lesson Idea

Use page 13 & 14 of **Captain Joe Saves the Day** as a reference for this lesson (makes reference to swampy pit thoughts).

Start the lesson out with an interactive brainstorming session to get the flow of ideas started for students regarding "swampy" thoughts and "happy" thoughts.

Write the ideas on the board for students to use as a reference for their T-Chart. Students will fill in a T-Chart (please see Activity Sheets section for handout) listing thoughts they have that belong in the swampy pit, e.g. "I can't do it". "He/she does it better", "I won't be good at that" etc.

This is a great place to remind learners that thoughts that belong in the swampy pit are the kinds of thoughts they can ZAP away with their own thought-zapping wands.

Students will fill in the other side of the T- Chart listing the thoughts they have that are happy and make them feel good, e.g. "I will try my best", "I am good at that", "I have fun", "I like to try" etc.

Closure

Activities #1, 2 & 3 were designed to help children learn about the importance of choosing happy thoughts to help protect their dreams, as opposed to falling into the trap of choosing thoughts that are self-limiting and can eventually become a part of their belief systems.

In Activity # 3, students will have an opportunity to fill in a sheet that gives a great visual of this concept, i.e. zapping swampy thoughts, and choosing happy thoughts to protect our dreams.

In Activity #3 students will need their two most common swampy thoughts and two most common happy thoughts.

So, a great closure activity for Activity #1, would be a class-share of their completed t-charts as well as giving students some extra time to circle two thoughts in their swampy thoughts list and two thoughts in their happy thoughts list that either: a) happen most often b) are their favorite.

Assessment
Please See Activity Sheets Section for Rubric

Activity #2 - Language Arts, Art

MY DREAM IS...

Lesson Objective/Outcome
To get students thinking about what is important to them. To set the stage so students begin feeling more confident in their abilities to reach their dreams and believe in themselves.

Preparation and Resources
Read **Captain Joe Saves the Day** to the class.
This lesson should be taught before Activity #3.

See Page 50 of Activity Sheets Section for the handout.

Lesson Idea

<u>HOOK:</u> Initiate Class Discussion with some kind of Soccer related item to represent Joe's Dream of becoming an excellent soccer goalie.

Another option is for you the teacher to bring in some kind of artifact that represents a dream or goal you have had as a child, an adult or perhaps something you are working on currently to engage the students in the topic of dreams and goals.

After a class discussion recapping Joe's dream of becoming a soccer goalie and the importance of having dreams and goals to strive for, students take part in an A/B Partner Talk to share some of their own dreams they have for the future.

After A/B Partner Share students will receive handouts to write down one sentence, or point form (depending on age level and ability) describing the dream/goal they want the most.

Students use pencil crayons, stickers or paint to decorate their dream heart.

Display finished Dream Hearts on Bulletin Board titled, "Our Dreams for the Future". Also display the captions "Believe in yourself!" and "You can reach your dreams!"

IDEA

Closure

Class share,

Option 1: students share what their top dream is with the class.

Option 2: Students share what their partner's top dream is with the class.

Assessment

Please See Activity Sheets Section for Rubric

Activity #3 - Language Arts

PROTECT YOUR DREAMS

Lesson Objective/Outcome
To "begin" developing an understanding of how our thoughts can either help us reach our dreams or how they can sometimes prevent us from reaching our dreams.

Preparation and Resources
This lesson should be taught after Activity #1 and #2 and after Captain Joe Saves the Day has been read to the class.

See Page 51 in Activity Sheets Section for the handout.

Students will use their information from the first two Activities to complete this handout.

Lesson Idea
Pages 21 & 22 of **Captain Joes Saves the Day** provides a great Hook or reference for this lesson (illustration of Joe zapping swampy pit thought as soon as it happened).

Generate a class discussion based on Joe's experience of discovering ways to help protect his dream of becoming a great Soccer Goalie (i.e. ZAP his swampy thoughts as soon as they happen and replace them with happy thoughts).

A/B Partner talk, to share an experience when they may have let a thought get in the way of doing something or getting something they wanted.

Each student will receive a handout. They will pick their top 2 swampy pit thoughts and top 2 happy thoughts that they circled in Activity #1 and fill it in the appropriate spot on the handout. They will also re-write their top Dream/goal from Activity #2 in the appropriate spot on the handout.

This handout provides a great visual for students and could be used as a tool and positive reminder to believe in themselves.

Closure

Great Opportunity for Students to do a mini-presentation describing their dream/goal and the ways they are going to help protect their dream (i.e. "Zapping these swampy thoughts..." "Choosing these happy thoughts...")

Assessment

Please See Rubric in Activity Sheets Section

Activity #4 - Performing Arts

CAPTAIN JOE SAVES THE DAY TABLEAU

Lesson Objective/Outcome

To participate in a drama activity to explore the roles of the Captain Joe characters.

Preparation and Resources

This lesson should be taught after **Captain Joe Saves the Day** has been read to the class.

See Page 52 in Activity Sheets Section for the handout.

Set up a clear safe space for the children, ideal for the gymnasium.

Lesson Idea

The class will be divided into groups to perform 5 separate tableau scenes (i.e. story plot moments) that represent the **Captain Joe Saves the Day** story.

Practice what some of the more difficult actions may look like, and give an overview of what a tableau is ~ a freeze frame of a scene from the story. Students will be in character representing the scene and the teacher will sound a chime or some kind of signal and the students will "freeze" to create a standstill picture.

Arrange students in groups of 4 or 5 (depending on the size of the classroom). The teacher will narrate the tableau scenes while the students perform.

After students have been organized into groups, the teacher could work independently with each group to make sure they all understand the events and expressions in the scene. Other groups could be practicing their scene or working on another activity, such as silent reading, while teacher is giving direction to individual groups.

Students will perform their tableaus in sequence. Classmates act as audience members when they are not performing.

Closure

Question and answering period, each group will have the opportunity to answer any questions or comments their classmates may have about the scene they performed.

Each group could say they are going to answer "x" number of questions/comments).

Assessment

Please See Rubric in Activity Sheets Section.

Activity #5 - Art

CREATE A PICTURE

Lesson Objective/Outcome
For students to create an image of the story using elements of art.

Preparation and Resources
The **Captain Joe Saves the Day** story will have been read to the class.

Pencils, Paint

See Page 53 in Activity Sheets Section for the handout.

Lesson Idea
Choose your favorite part of the story, **Captain Joe Saves the Day**.

Draw a picture of your favorite part and then paint the picture. Write a sentence telling why this is your favorite part.

Closure
Give students the opportunity to share their finished pictures with their classmates.

Assessment
Please See Rubric in Activity Sheets Section

Activity #6 - Writing Activity, Language Arts

LIVING MY DREAM

Lesson Objective/Outcome
To think about and write down what it would be like to achieve their dream.

Preparation and Resources
Captain Joe Saves the Day, will have been read to the class.

Pencils, Paper

Lesson Idea

Use page 17 & 18 of **Captain Joe Saves the Day** as a reference for this lesson.

Imagine you have reached your dream, just like Joe did in the story when he zapped himself into the future and was actually the star goalie out on the field.

Write down what a day in the life of you dream would be like.

Option: Students might need some sentence starters or ideas, some examples: What would you do when you woke up in the morning? How would you feel? Who else would be there with you? What would you say?

Closure
Give students an opportunity to share their stories with each other.

Assessment
Please See Rubric in Activity Sheets Section

ACTIVITY SHEETS FOR CAPTAIN JOE SAVES THE DAY

Captain
Joe
Saves the
Day!

Captain: _____
Your Name

Comprehension:

1) What is Joe's favorite thing to play?

2) What position did Joe dream of being really great at?

3) Joe used his thought-zapping _____ to help protect his dreams.

Word Study:

1) Add "s", "ed", and "ing" to the end of the following words:

a) play   b) pick   c) glow   d) want

2) Add **er** and **est** to the end of the following words:

a) long   b) happy   c) early   d) dark

Hint: **Remember to change the "y" to "i" before adding the ending

Something to think about:

What do you dream of doing?

Captain: _____
(Your name)

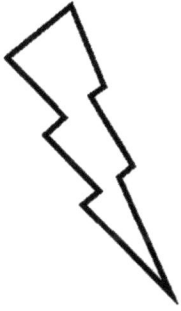

Swampy Pit Thoughts

Happy Thoughts

One of my dreams is:

_____

_____

_____

_____

_____

Captain: _____

(your name)

My swampy pit thoughts I ZAP are:

_____

_____

_____

Captain: _____
(Your name)

A happy thought I use to protect my dream is:

_____

_____

One of my dreams is:

_____

_____

_____

A happy thought I use to protect my dream is:

_____

_____

Tableau Scenes for Captain Joe Saves the Day:

1) Joe and his classmates were standing in a circle around Mrs.Donnelly. Everyone looked happy as Mrs.Donnelly held out a soccer ball and announced they would playing be soccer. Joe raises his arm as he very happily yells "All Right!" (Positions: Joe, Mrs.Donnelly, Classmates).

2) Joe couldn't overcome the dark swampy pit thought; it hung heavily around him like a storm cloud as he very sadly walked home. (Positions: Joe, as many students as possible representing a dark, heavy cloud ~ students could have their arms arched over Joe like they are overpowering him).

3) Joe was zapped into the future as a STAR soccer goalie, he crouched down in front of the net looking strong and happy as his fans were chanting and cheering for him in the background. (Positions: Joe, Fans)

4) Joe discovered it's important to protect his dreams. Joe pulled out his wand and ZAPPED the Dark swampy thoughts away! (Positions: Joe pointing his wand, as many students as possible representing a dark grouchy looking cloud).

5) Joe and his classmates had the time of their lives playing a fun game of soccer, and of course Joe was the goalie! (Positions: Joe, Classmates).

Idea: If available, blocks or chairs could be used to represent soccer net.

My Favorite Part of Captain Joe Saves the Day!

_____

_____

_____

_____

Vocabulary for spelling tests

any   long

ball   love

fan   pout

game   tell

heart   you

* **Please note**: The above words are intended to be used, one or two at a time, as an addition to weekly spelling tests or as an addition to the Word Wall. The words range in difficulty level from moderate to more complicated.

Captain Joe Saves the Day Word Search

```
G N H Z T Y N E V H D T L J B
Y O U R U Z B L O N G A L B A
X H A J A M Y J N Q S N A U V
H E T P D K N C K P D A B R Y
H C G Q L D D K V Y Y V N N P
T D N C O X L B A A Z J W R U
Y H F I V B L A Q F K W P N B
G L E V E D E N P Q T R N M U
C R E M A G T Y X U G R E E N
K B A D S N W C K U D I A R M
U K F X L D Z P H C W A H E S
L A E J Y M P O U T D O P C B
N Z L S S L C Y X J A L V C P
Q V E G U K O Y N V S Q G O P
L G C K M B G E O Z E P C S F
```

Look for Words: frontward, backward & diagnal

ANY	GAME	LONG	SOCCER
BALL	GREEN	LOVE	TELL
FAN	HEART	POUT	YOU

Captain Joe Saves the Day Story Sequence

Beginning	Middle	End

  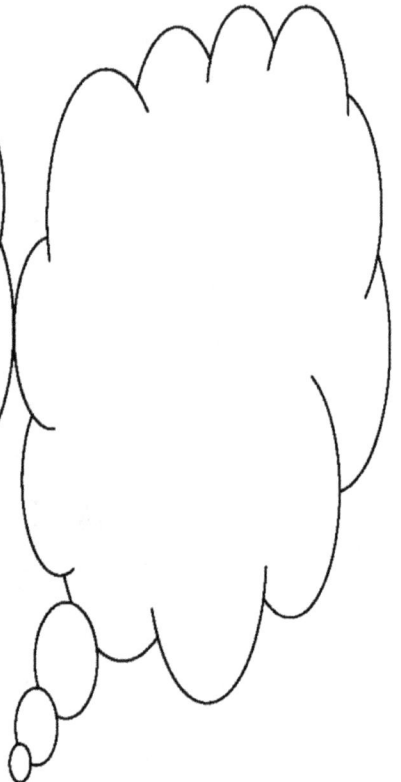

In the Beginning: In the Middle: In the End:

Captain Joe Saves the Day Story Sequence (Adapted Version)

Beginning	Middle	End

In the Beginning:	In the Middle:	In the End:

Subtract the numbers in each box to discover what the message below says.

B   10
     - 5
 ------------ 	
	E 8
	     - 2
	 ------------ 	
		F 15
		     - 4
		 ------------ 	

I   17
     - 2
 ------------ 	
	L 9
	     - 5
	 ------------ 	
		N 17
		     - 3
		 ------------ 	

O   19
     - 7
 ------------ 	
	R 12
	    - 10
	 ------------ 	
		S 4
		     - 3
		 ------------ 	

U   9
     - 2
 ------------ 	
	V 7
	     - 4
	 ------------ 	
		Y 15
		     - 2
		 ------------ 	

___   ___   ___   ___   ___   ___   ___
 5   6   4   15   6   3   6

___   ___
15   14

___   ___   ___   ___   ___   ___   ___   ___ !
13   12   7   2   1   6   4   11

Subtract the numbers in each box to discover what the message below says.

B   10
    - 5
 -------------- 	
     5
	E 8
	    - 2
	 ------------- 	
	     6
		F 15
		    - 4
		 -------------- 	
		    11

I   17
    - 2
 -------------- 	
    15
	L 9
	    - 5
	 -------------- 	
	     4
		N 17
		    - 3
		 -------------- 	
		    14

O   19
    - 7
 -------------- 	
    12
	R 12
	    - 10
	 -------------- 	
	     2
		S 4
		    - 3
		 -------------- 	
		     1

U   9
    - 2
 -------------- 	
     7
	V 7
	    - 4
	 -------------- 	
	     3
		Y 15
		    - 2
		 -------------- 	
		    13

B   E   L   I   E   V   E

I   N

Y   O   U   R   S   E   L   F!

Assessment Rubrics

Assessment, Lesson 1

Outcome	Criteria				Total
	1 (Not yet)	2 (Meets)	3 (Fully Meets)	4 (Exceeds)	
Create a T-Chart with 3 or more thought ideas on both sides of the chart	Did not have thought ideas on both sides of the chart	Had at least 2 thought ideas on **each** side of the chart	Had 3 or more thought ideas on each side of the chart	Had 3 or more thought ideas on each side of the chart, and at least half were original answers not on the board	

Assessment, Lesson 2

Outcome	Criteria				Total
	1 (Not yet)	2 (Meets)	3 (Fully Meets)	4 (Exceeds)	
Demonstrate good speaking & listening skills during A/B Partner share so each partner is able to generate their own "dream" ideas that will be used to complete a writing task.	Did not stay on task to generate ideas - either didn't listen or share with their partner.	Stayed on task most of the time, took a bit of encouraging and reminding to either listen or share with their partner, came up with ideas in the end.	Stayed on task during A/B partner share, both partners generated ideas for writing task.	Stayed on task during A/B partner share, encouraged one another and/or asked questions about partner's ideas, both partners generated ideas for writing task.	

Assessment, Lesson 3

Outcome	Criteria				Total
	1 (Not yet)	2 (Meets)	3 (Fully Meets)	4 (Exceeds)	
Fully Complete handout, which will be used as a tool to remind students to believe in themselves.	All three sections of handout incomplete.	Wrote some ideas in each of the 3 sections, 1 or more section complete	Completed all 3 sections on the handout, i.e. 2 swampy thoughts, 2 happy thoughts and 1 dream	Completed all 3 sections on the handout and added more than 2 swampy/happy thoughts	

Assessment, Lesson 4

Outcome	Criteria				Total
	1 (Not yet)	2 (Meets)	3 (Fully Meets)	4 (Exceeds)	
Work cooperatively with group members to create a group tableau scene	Unwilling to work in a group dynamic	Worked cooperatively with group members and stayed on task most of the time	Worked cooperatively with group members and contributed ideas to create tableau scene	Worked cooperatively with group members and acted as a positive leader in creation of tableau scene	

Assessment, Lesson 5

Outcome	Criteria				Total
	1 (Not yet)	2 (Meets)	3 (Fully Meets)	4 (Exceeds)	
Complete drawing of favorite part of story, paint drawing and write one sentence to describe it	Did not complete drawing, painting or written description.	Completed drawing and written description but did not paint the picture.	Completed drawing, painted the drawing and wrote one sentence to describe it	Completed drawing, painted the drawing and wrote more than one sentence to describe it	

Assessment, Lesson 6

Outcome	Criteria				Total
	1 (Not yet)	2 (Meets)	3 (Fully Meets)	4 (Exceeds)	
Demonstrate good speaking/presenting skills during class share of story	Was unwilling to participate in presenting their story	Willing to participate in presenting, could have spoke clearer and did not make eye contact with the audience	Willing to participate in presenting, spoke clearly and made eye contact	Willing to participate in presenting, spoke clearly, made eye contact and asked the audience if they had questions	

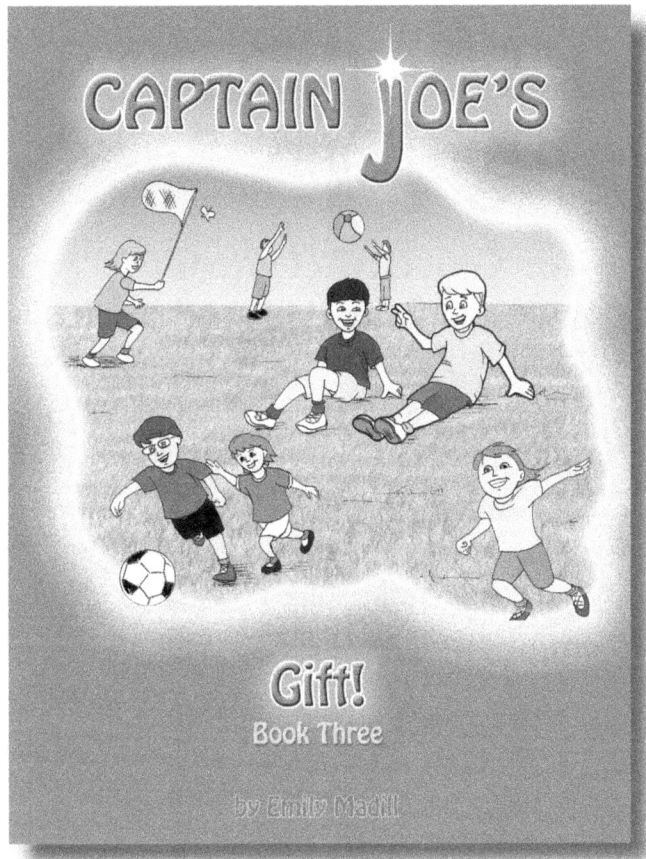

Using the books in the classroom:

The following six activities, based on the story **Captain Joe's Gift**, are intended for a Grade 1 - Grade 3 level of learners, specifically targeting grade 2.

Handouts for the lessons can be found in the Activity Sheets Section. The Activity Sheets Section also contains a Story Sequence handout, Math handout, Word Search, and Spelling Vocabulary List.

There is also a "Comprehension, Word Study and Something to Think About" worksheet in the Activity Sheets section. The Something to Think About question could either be used as a journal writing activity, or the back of the handout could be used for students to write a longer answer.

Rubrics have been created for 4 of the 6 lessons as an assessment tool. These Rubrics could be adapted to suit the particular needs of your class. They could also be altered to assess a different learning outcome than the one stated.

MY SPECIAL GIFT

Lesson Objective/Outcome

To create a list of what students believe their own special gifts are. To become more secure in their ability to define who they are and what is important to them.

Preparation and Resources

HOOK: KWL Chart, give students an opportunity to reflect on what they know from the last two books, make some predictions about this book and plant the seed for students to begin thinking about what their own special gifts and abilities are.

Read, **Captain Joe's Gift** to the class.

Piece of paper for draft copy.

See Page 77 in Activity Sheets Section for the handout.

Lesson Idea

Use pages 17 & 18 of **Captain Joe's Gift** as a reference for this lesson.

Students work independently to write down as many things down as they can that they feel they are good at and/or they enjoy doing (brainstorm ideas without worrying about spelling, neatness etc.). It's important for the children to come up with their ideas on their own (crate an atmosphere so they are not comparing their ideas with their neighbor's ideas). If a student is really struggling to come up with ideas, teacher can use scaffolding to help them reach their own realization of what they feel they are good at and enjoy doing.

After students have a list of ideas, they can go through and look for themes of ideas that are very similar, i.e. love baseball, good at throwing balls, good at catching balls – special gift could be "I am athletic" or "I am a great baseball player". Students will then pick their favorite idea to write down as one of their special gifts.

Give students handouts to write down what one of their special gifts is.

Closure

Students can decorate their Special Gift Ribbons, using pencil crayons, paint, stickers etc. Class share, each student is given the opportunity to share what one of their special gifts is.

Adaptation

Teacher/adult can use scaffolding to help children who are struggling with creating ideas.

Assessment

Please See Rubric in Activity Sheets Section.

Activity #2 - Language Arts

SPECIAL GIFT CONFIDENCE BOOSTER

Lesson Objective/Outcome

To boost children's confidence. To have an exercise that can be used on a regular basis for children to honour themselves and their classmates for their unique abilities and special gifts.

Preparation and Resources

This lesson should be taught after Activity #1 and after students have heard the story, **Captain Joe's Gift.**

See Page 78 in Activity Sheets Section for the handout.

Lesson Idea

Teacher will use the ideas that students came up with in Activity #1 to fill in a "Special Gift Award" for each student (plan it so students don't know).

Gather Children in the reading area and organize them so they are all sitting in a circle where they can see one another.

Let the children know how proud you are of each and every one of them and how honoured you feel to have such a great group of students with such unique and equally special gifts. Let them know that they will each be receiving an award for "one" of their "many" special gifts. Tell them this is a celebration and each person will receive applause from everyone.

If this becomes a regular and comfortable exercise, students could take turns sitting in the middle of the circle while they are being honoured.

Hand out awards to each student and ensure they have equal time being honoured.

Closure

Give students an opportunity to decorate their awards with pencil crayons, crayons and stickers.

Collect Awards to be used as a regular "Confidence Building Exercise"

Follow the same "award ceremony circle" format as this activity to create a regular routine of building confidence and honouring one another for being special.

IDEA

Option

After each student is honoured, you could ask them if there is another special gift they have that they would like to share (and then add it to their award for the next ceremony). As this exercise becomes familiar, students may feel more comfortable and safe sharing their many special gifts with their classmates (this is a great opportunity for students to "determine" and "express" what their gifts are).

Activity #3 - Language Arts, Art

PERSONALIZED MINI-BOOK

Lesson Objective/Outcome
For students to create their own resource for boosting their confidence.

Preparation and Resources
This lesson should be taught after Activity #1 and after students have heard the story, **Captain Joe's Gift.**

See Page 79 in Activity Sheets Section for the Mini-Book handout.

Scissors
Pencils, pencil crayons/crayons
Optional: Blank/scrap paper

Lesson Idea

Use The Front Book Cover of **Captain Joe's Gift** as a reference/hook for this lesson.

Students will create their own mini-book that can be used as a great tool for boosting their belief in themselves.

The book will include:
A Cover, they will fill their own names in the line provided (Captain _____'s Gift), they will also draw a picture on the cover to represent themselves and one of their gifts.

Optional: Blank/scrap paper can be added after each of the main pages for illustrations that will represent their special gifts, happy thoughts etc.

A Page where they will list some of their Special Gifts.

A Page where they will list one of their Dreams/goals.

A Page where they will list some of their happy thoughts and some of their unhappy thoughts for zapping.

Students will use scissors to cut along the dotted lines. After information is filled in and pictures and colour have been added, the books should be stapled.

Closure

Create a space for students to display their books, perhaps in the classroom reading area or library.

Assessment

Please See Rubric in Activity Sheets Section.

Activity #4 - Art, Language Arts

HONOURING ONE ANOTHER

Lesson Objective/Outcome
To provide children with the message that it is wonderful we are all able to be special and unique for different reasons. To give students an opportunity to practice honouring others for their special gifts, as well as receiving acceptance for their own special gifts.

Preparation and Resources
Blank Paper
Pencils, Pencil Crayons/Paint/Crayons

Lesson Idea

Use Page 21 as a reference or hook for the lesson.

Start the lesson off with a recap of page 24 and Joe's message: "You are always telling me it's important to feel happy with who we are. When we try to be something we are not, we can make others around us feel like they should be different that they are too."

Arrange students in partners.

A/B Partner share, each student will have an opportunity to share with the other what their own special gift(s) is.

Students will then work independently to create a picture representing their partner's special gift and a sentence to describe it.

Students will add an art element to decorate their pictures.

Closure

A/B Partner share, each student will give their finished pictures to their partners and give their partner a verbal compliment to honour them for their special gift.

Assessment

Please See Rubric in Activity Sheets Section.

Activity #5 - Performing Arts

MY SPECIAL GIFT ACTION

Lesson Objective/Outcome
To give students the opportunity to further solidify their belief in themselves and their special gift(s).

Preparation and Resources
This activity requires a clear space, ideal for the gymnasium.

This lesson should be taught after the first couple of activities and after students have heard the story, **Captain Joe's Gift**.

Lesson Idea
Students will have an opportunity to put a physical action to represent one of their special gifts. Some examples, If writing is a special gift, then the student could pretend they are writing on a pad of paper, or if a student is a fast runner, they could run on the spot. The idea is for them to come up with an action that can be displayed safely in one spot.
Students could work in pairs to come up with their actions.

After everyone has an action they are comfortable with, arrange students in one big circle. Students will have the opportunity to 1) Say what their special gift is and 2) will show classmates the action. Then as a class, students will say e.g. "Jack's special gift is throwing and then will mimic Jack's action". This will continue until everyone has had an opportunity to share.

Teacher could start the circle by sharing one of his/her special gifts and actions. Another idea, to make students feel more comfortable sharing they could recite their gift and action with their partner.

Closure

This activity could also be used as a memory exercise. After students have had the opportunity to go through their actions and their classmates a few times, the activity could be changed to a memory game.

One person starts by saying (ideal for instructor to start): "I am Brianna and my gift is listening" (perhaps action is putting hand to ear), and then everyone says Brianna's gift is listening while they do the appropriate action. Then the next student says, "I am Tom and my gift is helping others" (perhaps action is putting both hands out to offer a helping hand), and then everyone says, Brianna's gift is listening, Tom's gift is helping others and on and on until everyone has had an opportunity to add to the chain.

Activity #6 - Art

CREATE A PICTURE

Lesson Objective/Outcome
For students to create an image of the story using elements of art.

Preparation and Resources
Captain Joe's Gift will have been read to the class.

Pencils, Paint

See Page 80 in Activity Sheets Section for the handout.

Lesson Idea
Choose your favorite part of the story, **Captain Joe's Gift**.

Draw a picture of your favorite part and then paint the picture. Write a sentence telling why this is your favorite part.

Closure
Give students the opportunity to share their finished pictures with their classmates.

IDEA   Mount on construction paper

Assessment
Please See Rubric in Activity Sheets Section

ACTIVITY SHEETS FOR CAPTAIN JOE'S GIFT

Captain Joe's Gift

Captain: _____
Your Name

<u>Comprehension</u>:

1) What is Joe's little brother's name?

2) Who is Joe's friend that has a gift of being funny?

3) What is Joe's special gift?

<u>Word Study</u>:

Change the <u>first letter</u> of each of these words to make a new word.

a) fun   b) had   c) go   d) take

<u>Match</u> the words that <u>rhyme</u> with each other

a) pool   b) say   c) can   d) cool   e) ran f) play

<u>Something to think about</u>:

One of My Special Gifts is:

_____

_____

_____

Captain: _____
(Your name)

This SPECIAL GIFT Award
goes to: _____

For your Special Gift of:

_____

_____

_____

This SPECIAL GIFT Award
goes to: _____

For your Special Gift of:

_____

_____

_____

Captain _____'s Gift!

Unhappy Thoughts I ZAP!:

Happy Thoughts I Choose:

One of My Dreams is to:

Some of my Special Gifts are:

Captain: _____

(Your name)

My Favorite Part of Captain Joe's Gift

_____

_____

_____

_____

_____

80

Vocabulary for spelling tests

Charlie	help
fun	hot
glad	special
good	sure
Jake	why

* Please note: The above words are intended to be used, one or two at a time, as an addition to weekly spelling tests or as an addition to the Word Wall. The words range in difficulty level from moderate to more complicated.

Captain Joe's Gift Word Search

```
E H I J O G L T F K O E U F Z
Q I C E W L T I U I U A S U N
E T L A Q A K J N M X P M Q G
H R T R E D F W P P E L X M G
Q B U A A T R S C C M X J L S
Q G S S H H C P I Y H C S L F
H K R Z X W C A K M M L J B V
G Q O P F W L W J S M L V F T
P L E H T G H W I B D X V Y R
H A P O L R H Y L G S Y M F H
V O V D Y A D Y J G T W I D L
X V T X K C F O T E Z W I U Z
S A I T U I B S O M A J E M A
B P P W H E O V X G K D B S L
Q R S K F Y E N V M O G X Q K
```

Look for Words: frontward, backward & diagnal

CHARLIE	**GOOD**	**SPECIAL**	**SWIM**
FUN	**HELP**	**SUN**	**TEACH**
GLAD	**HOT**	**SURE**	**WHY**

Captain Joe's Gift Story Sequence

Beginning	Middle	End

  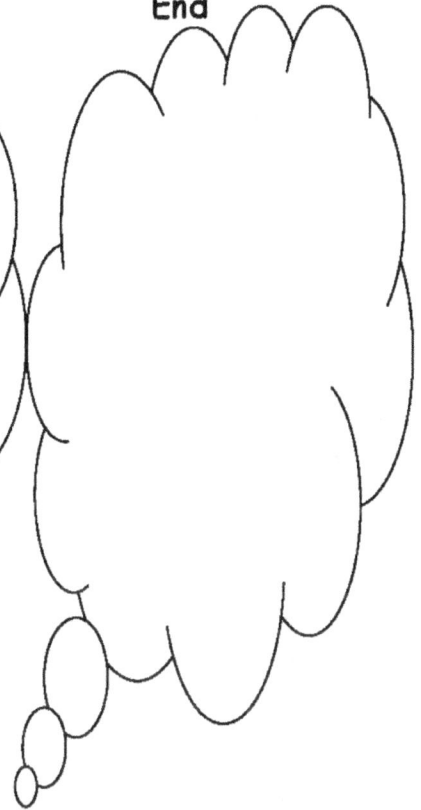

In the Beginning:

In the Middle:

In the End:

Captain Joe's Gift Story Sequence (Adapted Version)

Beginning

Middle

End

In the Beginning:	In the Middle:	In the End:

Mathematics

__Add__ the numbers in each box to discover what the message below says.

A 24 + 3 --------------	C 12 + 2 --------------	E 27 + 1 --------------	I 51 + 6 --------------
L 15 + 4 --------------	O 93 + 5 --------------	P 88 + 1 --------------	R 40 + 2 --------------

S 12 + 6 --------------	U 34 + 5 --------------	Y 33 + 3 --------------

$$\overline{}\ \overline{}\ \overline{}\ \overline{}\ \overline{}\ \overline{}$$

36   98   39   27   42   28

18   98

18   89   28   14   57   27   19 !

Add the numbers in each box to discover what the message below says.

A   24
   + 3
------------- 	
27
	C 12
	   + 2
	------------- 	
	14
		E 27
		   + 1
		------------- 	
		28
			I 51
			   + 6
			------------- 	
			57

L   15
   + 4
------------- 	
19
	O 93
	   + 5
	------------- 	
	98
		P 88
		   + 1
		------------- 	
		89
			R 40
			   + 2
			------------- 	
			42

S   12
   + 6
------------- 	
18
	U 34
	   + 5
	------------- 	
	39
		Y 33
		   + 3
		------------- 	
		36

Y O U   A R E

S O

S P E C I A L!

Assessment Rubrics

Assessment, Lesson 1

Outcome	Criteria				Total
	1 (Not yet)	2 (Meets)	3 (Fully Meets)	4 (Exceeds)	
Demonstrate good speaking/presenting skills during class share of special gift ribbon	Was unwilling to participate in presenting their special gift ribbon	Willing to participate in presenting, could have spoke clearer and did not make eye contact with the audience	Willing to participate in presenting, spoke clearly and made eye contact	Willing to participate in presenting, spoke clearly, made eye contact and asked the audience if they had questions	

Assessment, Lesson 3

Outcome	Criteria				Total
	1 (Not yet)	2 (Meets)	3 (Fully Meets)	4 (Exceeds)	
Complete all 4 pages of their mini-book	Left one or more pages of their mini-book blank	All 4 pages have information filled in, some pages partially not fully complete	All four pages fully complete, front cover coloured	All four pages fully complete, front cover coloured, extra pages with illustrations have been added	

Assessment, Lesson 4

Outcome	Criteria				Total
	1 (Not yet)	2 (Meets)	3 (Fully Meets)	4 (Exceeds)	
Demonstrate good listening skills during A/B Partner Talk	Unwilling to participate in A/B Partner talk	Willing to take turns listening, but interrupted or spoke out of turn	Listened without speaking while partner shared	Listened without speaking while partner shared and also paraphrased something back to partner that he/she said	

Assessment, Lesson 6

Outcome	Criteria				Total
	1 (Not yet)	2 (Meets)	3 (Fully Meets)	4 (Exceeds)	
Demonstrate good speaking/presenting skills during class share of picture	Was unwilling to participate in presenting their picture	Willing to participate in presenting, could have spoke clearer and did not make eye contact with the audience	Willing to participate in presenting, spoke clearly and made eye contact	Willing to participate in presenting, spoke clearly, made eye contact and asked the audience if they had questions	

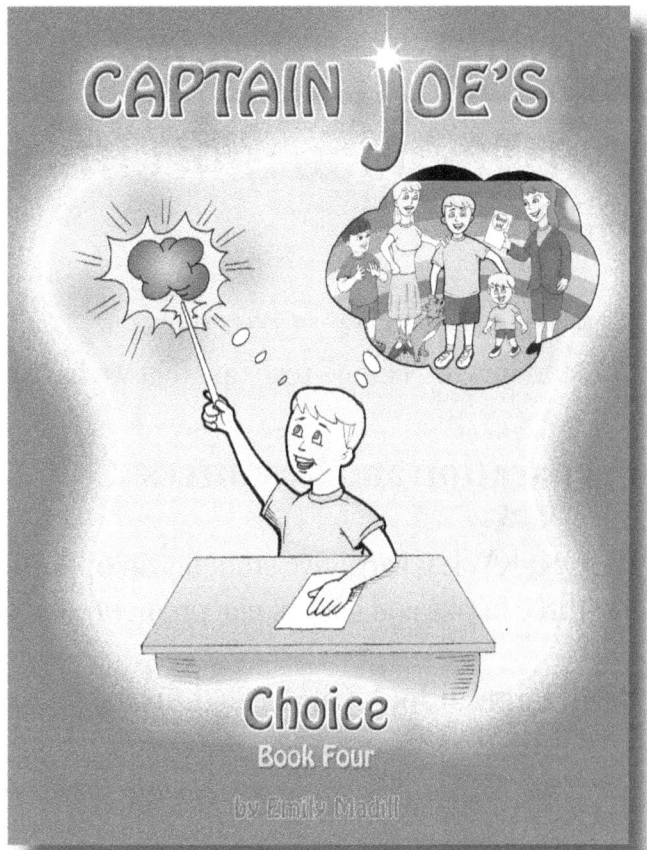

Using the books in the classroom:

The following six activities, based on the story **Captain Joe's Choice**, are intended for a Grade 2 - Grade 3 level of learners, specifically targeting grade 2.

Handouts for the lessons can be found in the Activity Sheets Section. The Activity Sheets Section also contains a Story Sequence handout, Math handout, Word Search, and Spelling Vocabulary List.

There is also a "Comprehension, Word Study and Something to Think About" worksheet in the Activity Sheets section. The Something to Think About question could either be used as a journal writing activity, or the back of the handout could be used for students to write a longer answer.

Rubrics have been created for each of the 6 lessons as an assessment tool. These Rubrics could be adapted to suit the particular needs of your class. They could also be altered to assess a different learning outcome than the one stated.

Activity #1 - Language Arts

UNHAPPY MOOD THOUGHTS VS. HAPPY MOOD THOUGHTS T-CHART

Lesson Objective/Outcome

For students to "begin" realizing that we have the ability to choose our thoughts.

Preparation and Resources

HOOK: KWL Chart, give students an opportunity to reflect on what they know from the last three books and make some predictions about this book.

Read, **Captain Joe's Choice** to the class.

See Page 103 in Activity Sheets Section for the handout.

Lesson Idea

Use pages 1 & 2 of **Captain Joe's Choice** as a reference for this lesson.

Class brainstorming session to come up with some collective ideas about unhappy mood thoughts and happy mood thoughts.

Use page 1 of the story as an idea starter for the brainstorming session.

Ask students to think about a time when they have had a rotten day where everything seems to go wrong and the more they think about the things not going their way the worse the day gets. Ask them to try to remember what that felt like and what kind of thoughts they were thinking.

Allow time for students to write down some ideas, or do this together as a group and write the ideas on the board.

Do the same thing, using reference to how they felt on a really happy day where everything seemed to get better and better.

Allow time for students to write down some ideas, or do this together as a group and write the ideas on the board.

Give students handouts.

Students will fill in their t-charts using their own ideas as well as the ones from the class brainstorming session.

Closure
Students could do a class share of their finished t-charts.

Assessment
Please See Rubric in Activity Sheets Section.

Activity #2 - Language Arts, Art

MY HAPPY MOOD MOVIE

Lesson Objective/Outcome
To begin to understand that when we make room for happy thoughts we feel better and have a happier time with others around us.

Preparation and Resources
See Page 104 in Activity Sheets Section for the handout.

Pencils, Pencil Crayons/Crayons

Lesson Idea

Use pages 15 & 16 of **Captain Joe's Choice** as a reference for this lesson.

Give students handouts, lead students through the following:

When Joe ZAPPED away all of his grumpy thoughts about the rotten start to his day he started to feel better. The better he felt, the happier he became until everything in his day turned around and he was having a great day.

Think about how you feel when having a really great day where you are in a very happy mood. What kinds of things would you do? Who would you be with?

Have students pause here and draw a picture of themselves experiencing their happy mood. Let them know, like Joe they get to be in their own happy mood movie in their drawing.

After students have completed their drawing, they will write either in point form or in sentence form a description of what happened in their happy mood movie and/or what kind of thoughts or feelings they experienced.

Closure

Students can add colour to their movies. Give students the opportunity to share their completed drawing and description.

Post finished drawings on display around the classroom and have a Happy Mood Movie Viewing" as a class. Class gathers around each picture while the student has an opportunity to talk about their happy mood movie (perhaps what they were doing, or thinking, or 2 things that made it happy etc.)

Assessment

Please See Rubric in Activity Sheets Section

Activity #3 - Performing Arts

NARRATIVE PANTOMIME

Lesson Objective/Outcome
To represent different moods associated with thoughts using a variety of movement and expression. To reinforce the concept that thoughts turn into things so choose thoughts that feel happy.

Preparation and Resources
This lesson should be taught after **Captain Joe's Choice** has been read to the class.

Set up a clear safe space for children, ideal for the gymnasium

See Page 105 in Activity Sheets Section for the handout.

Lesson Idea
Before starting the exercise, give students an orientation on the setting of the narrative pantomime.

IDEA Give students an opportunity to try out a few of the miming actions (e.g. zapping thoughts, picking up a garbage can). Remind them to be mindful of staying within their personal space, (size of space, dependent on location of exercise). Great idea for instructor to practice narrating the pantomime prior to using it with the class to see if there are any options to add light background music or sound effects.

Closure
Class discussion.

IDEA Topic of Discussion, discuss how easy it was for Joe to change his mind and feelings about his day and in doing so was able to recognize the opportunity to go enjoy his day with his friend Charlie.

Assessment
Please See Rubric in Activity Sheets Section

Activity #4 - Language Arts, Art

WHAT I HAVE LEARNED MINI-BOOK

Lesson Objective/Outcome
For students to create a summary of what they have learned from the 4 Captain Joe Books and Activities. Great opportunity for students to create evidence of their learning.

Preparation and Resources
This lesson should be taught after all of the four Captain Joe Series© books have been read to the students and after they have taken part in some activities to extend their learning of the concepts presented in the books.

See Page 106 in Activity Sheets Section for the Mini-Book handout.

Scissors
Pencils, pencil crayons/crayons

Lesson Idea
Students will create their own mini-book to summarize their learning and favorite parts of the 4 books.

The book will include:
A Cover, add their name to space and draw something in the box, e.g. their favorite Captain Joe book, what they have learned, their magic wand etc.

A Page where they write down the most important thing they have learned.

A Page where they write down which book was their favorite and why.

Students will use scissors to cut along the dotted lines. The books should be stapled after students have filled in their information and completed the front cover (with colour). Option: Instead of cutting the handout to make a book, students could fold the handout along the dotted line to make a book.

Closure

Give students opportunity to share their books with the class or with a partner.
Create a space for students to display their books, perhaps in the classroom reading area or library.

Assessment

Please See Rubric in Activity Sheets Section

Activity #5 - Language Arts

STORY WRITING

Lesson Objective/Outcome
Students will use their imaginations to write a new adventure for Joe and his thought-zapping superpower.

Preparation and Resources
This lesson should be taught after all of the four **Captain Joe Series**© books have been read to the students and after they have taken part in some activities to extend their learning of the concepts presented in the books.

Paper/journals, pencils

Lesson Idea
Students will create their own stories (length dependent on age and ability level).

This activity could take place during journal writing time.

Closure
Students could share their stories with a partner or the class.

Adaptation
Students could work in pairs to create the story.

Assessment
Please See Rubric in Activity Sheets Section

Activity #6 - Language Arts

STORY WRITING

Lesson Objective/Outcome
Students will use their imaginations to write an adventure about themselves and their own thought-zapping superpower.

Preparation and Resources
This lesson should be taught after all of the four **Captain Joe Series**© books have been read to the students and after they have taken part in some activities to extend their learning of the concepts presented in the books.

Paper, pencils

Lesson Idea
Students will create their own adventure where they are using their thought-zapping superpower in some way.

Students could add an illustration to their story. They could also create a mini-book with a cover, citing them as the author, and a back cover with a short "About the Author" write-up.

IDEA

Closure
Students could share their stories in partners or with the class. Finished work could be displayed on the Bulletin Board around the title:

"The Super Adventures of the Amazing Grade Twos"

Assessment
Please See Rubric in Activity Sheets Section

ACTIVITY SHEETS FOR CAPTAIN JOE'S CHOICE

Captain Joe's Choice

Captain: _____

Your name

Comprehension:

1) Name one reason why Joe was in a grouchy mood in the morning.

2) At the end of the story, did Joe **a) choose** to stay in an unhappy mood or
   b) choose to **zap** his thoughts and be in a happy mood?

3) Joe's adventure helped to show us why it is important to change our unhappy
   thoughts to _____ thoughts before they end up in the
   swampy pit.

Word Study:

A word that means more than one, one hat, two hat<u>s</u>, is called a <u>plural</u>.
Write the <u>plurals</u> of each of these words:

a) ball   b) boot   c) friend   d) sock

Make a word that is the <u>opposite</u> of each of these words:

a) happy   b) frown   c) big   d) outside

Something to think about:
If "**You**" wake up in a grouchy mood, will you use your invisible thought-zapping
wand? Why or why not?

Unhappy Mood Thoughts   **Happy Mood Thoughts**

Captain _____'s Happy Mood Movie

In my Happy Mood Movie I:

_____

_____

_____

Narrative Pantomime:

Captain Joe's thought journey...

It was a foggy autumn morning and the air had a chilly bite. Joe very sleepily <u>put on his coat</u> (PAUSE) then he <u>put on his gum boots, one after the other</u> (PAUSE). Today was a day off school, but it was also garbage day and it was Joe's turn to take out the garbage. Joe noticed the lid was off the big garbage can, so he <u>picked the heavy lid up and put it back on the garbage can</u> (PAUSE).

Ughh, he thought that is soooo gross! Joe thought about how he would rather be in his warm bed as he <u>lifted the big and very heavy garbage can</u> (PAUSE). This is not fair, the driveway is way too long thought Joe, as he <u>struggled to carry the heavy garbage can to the curb</u> (Pause). I have the day off school and now I have to do this!

Just then, Joe remembered his wand was in his boot. He very quickly <u>pulled his thought-zapping wand out of his gumboot</u> (PAUSE). He <u>raised his superpower wand in the air</u> (PAUSE) and he <u>ZAPPED</u> all of his grouchy, swampy thoughts.

Right away, the sun appeared and Joe noticed a bird chirping in the distance, he <u>tilted his head and put his hand to his ear</u> (PAUSE) to listen better. Joe <u>picked the garbage can back up</u> (PAUSE), only this time it didn't seem nearly as heavy. Now, he felt happy as he easily <u>carried the garbage can</u>. Before he knew it, Joe was at the end of the driveway. He <u>very easily put the garbage can down</u> (PAUSE) and then he <u>smiled</u>, hmmm that wasn't so bad he thought.

Then he thought, I didn't realize what a nice day it is, what will I do today?? Just then, Charlie rode up on his bike. Joe <u>smiled and waved his arms</u>, "Hey Charlie!" "What are you doing today?" Let's ride bikes yelled Charlie. "Sounds great!" said Joe. Joe's bike just happened to be on the front lawn so he excitedly <u>grabbed his bike and hopped on</u> (PAUSE). Joe wore a <u>giant smile as he rode off on his bike into the distance</u> (PAUSE) all the while thinking what a great day it had become since remembering to <u>ZAP</u> his grouchy thoughts.
~The End

<u>Note</u>: Underlined text represents the action students will mime. The "Pause" is there to give players enough time to mime the action.

Captain _____

The most important thing I learned from the Captain Joe Books is:

_____
_____
_____
_____
_____
_____

I am going to use my wand to:

My favorite Captain Joe book is

_____

It is my favorite because:

_____
_____
_____
_____
_____
_____

Vocabulary for spelling tests

boot	see
choose	snow
dog	Wally
foot	wet
gum	your

* Please note: The above words are intended to be used, one or two at a time, as an addition to weekly spelling tests or as an addition to the Word Wall. The words range in difficulty level from moderate to more complicated.

Captain Joe's Choice Word Search

```
A  I  F  X  Y  U  C  C  Q  V  F  Z  Y  O  M
P  I  O  U  X  W  U  O  S  V  U  F  C  G  U
Q  T  N  D  U  A  V  E  L  N  C  A  H  P  G
R  Z  N  O  X  I  T  R  S  D  O  T  Y  V  D
W  S  L  Z  U  A  M  W  B  M  J  W  P  Z  Q
O  O  X  O  R  N  D  Y  A  R  P  Y  V  W  J
X  K  D  X  S  A  K  V  V  H  S  U  E  M  U
F  W  Y  T  U  D  V  C  I  Y  X  S  P  V  P
T  V  G  O  Q  F  O  D  W  X  O  R  U  O  Y
B  T  R  S  I  H  G  F  O  W  V  V  T  M  M
C  C  M  O  L  U  R  D  H  S  A  K  E  T  T
J  E  O  R  A  T  S  C  R  R  L  W  R  O  Q
A  F  E  H  Y  R  R  J  U  C  L  V  O  F  W
H  E  J  S  C  S  R  V  B  B  Y  B  G  P  H
Y  Z  L  B  Z  F  Y  G  S  J  Q  R  B  S  S
```

Look for Words: frontward, backward & diagnal

BOOT	DOG	SEE	WALLY
CHOOSE	FOOT	SNOW	WET
COLD	GUM	STAR	YOUR

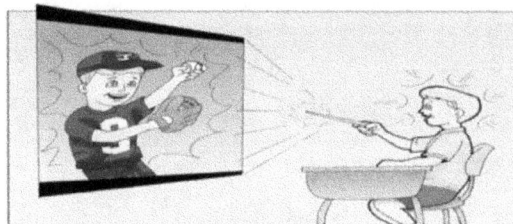

Captain Joe's Choice Story Sequence

| Beginning | Middle | End |

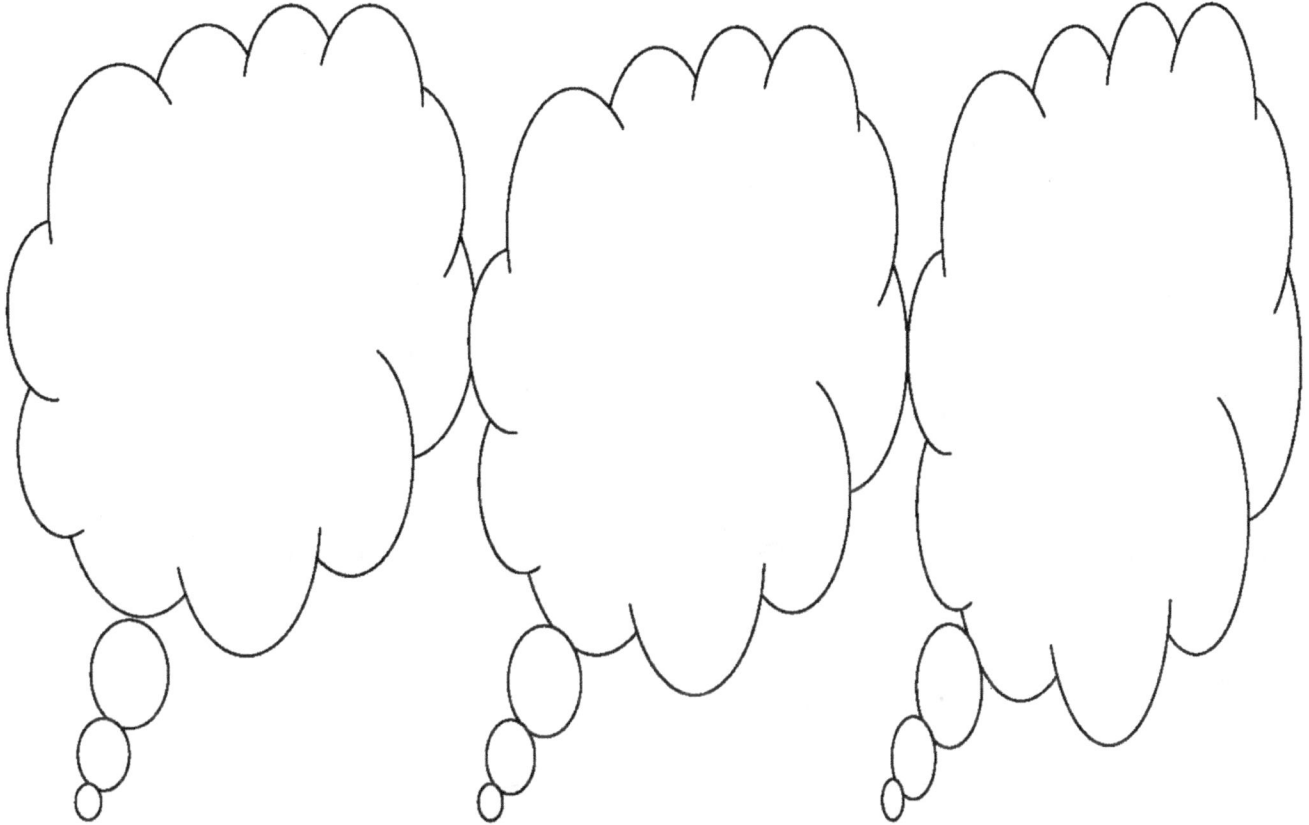

In the Beginning: In the Middle: In the End:

Captain Joe's Choice Story Sequence (Adapted Version)

Beginning   **Middle**   **End**

In the Beginning: In the Middle: In the End:

Mathematics

Add the numbers in each box to discover what the message below says.

A   24
  + 24
-------------- 	
	C 40
	  + 40
	-------------- 	
		E 46
		  + 53
		-------------- 	
			G 52
			  + 20
			-------------- 	

H   33
  + 14
-------------- 	
	O 10
	  + 50
	-------------- 	
		P 24
		  + 44
		-------------- 	
			R 61
			  + 27
			-------------- 	

S   30
  + 40
-------------- 	
	T 21
	  + 52
	-------------- 	
		U 23
		  + 52
		-------------- 	
			Y 14
			  + 13
			-------------- 	

___   ___   ___   ___   ___   ___
80   47   60   60   70   99

___ ___ ___ ___ ___ ___ ___ ___
73   47   60   75   72   47   73   70

___ ___ ___ ___   ___ ___ ___
73   47   48   73   48   88   99

___ ___ ___ ___ ___ !
47   48   68   68   27

Mathematics ~ Answer Key

Add the numbers in each box to discover what the message below says.

A 24 + 24 ------------ **48**	C 40 + 40 ------------ **80**	E 46 + 53 ------------ **99**	G 52 + 20 ------------ **72**
H 33 + 14 ------------ **47**	O 10 + 50 ------------ **60**	P 24 + 44 ------------ **68**	R 61 + 27 ------------ **88**
S 30 + 40 ------------ **70**	T 21 + 52 ------------ **73**	U 23 + 52 ------------ **75**	Y 14 + 13 ------------ **27**

C H O O S E

T H O U G H T S

T H A T   A R E

H A P P Y !

Assessment Rubrics

Assessment, Lesson 1

Outcome	Criteria				Total
	1 (Not yet)	2 (Meets)	3 (Fully Meets)	4 (Exceeds)	
Create a T-Chart with 3 or more thought ideas on both sides of the chart	Did not have thought ideas on both sides of the chart	Had at least 2 thought ideas on **each** side of the chart	Had 3 or more thought ideas on each side of the chart	Had 3 or more thought ideas on each side of the chart, and at least half were original answers not on the board	

Assessment, Lesson 2

Outcome	Criteria				Total
	1 (Not yet)	2 (Meets)	3 (Fully Meets)	4 (Exceeds)	
Complete drawing of their own happy mood movie, colour drawing and write one sentence to describe it	Did not complete drawing, add colour or written description.	Completed drawing and written description but did not add colour to the picture.	Completed drawing, added colour to the drawing and wrote one sentence to describe it	Completed drawing, added colour to the drawing and wrote more than one sentence to describe it	

Assessment, Lesson 3

Outcome	Criteria				Total
	1 (Not yet)	2 (Meets)	3 (Fully Meets)	4 (Exceeds)	
Demonstrate a willingness to participate in narrative pantomime and stayed on task for entire exercise	Was not willing to participate in narrative pantomime	Was willing to participate in narrative pantomime and stayed on task for most of the exercise	Was willing to participate in narrative pantomime and stayed on task for the entire exercise	Was willing to participate in narrative pantomime stayed on task for the entire exercise and contributed to class discussion after the exercise	

Assessment, Lesson 4

Outcome		Criteria			Total
	1 (Not yet)	2 (Meets)	3 (Fully Meets)	4 (Exceeds)	
Complete all 4 pages of their mini-book	Left one or more pages of their mini-book blank	All 4 pages have information filled in, some pages partially not fully complete	All four pages fully complete, front cover coloured	All four pages fully complete, more than 1 reason why in the favorite book section, front cover coloured, extra pages with illustrations have been added	

Assessment, Lesson 5

Outcome		Criteria			Total
	1 (Not yet)	2 (Meets)	3 (Fully Meets)	4 (Exceeds)	
Write a "**new**" adventure for Joe and his thought-zapping power that is 3 or more sentences long	Did not write a new adventure for Joe and his thought-zapping power	Wrote a story relating to Joe, but not a "**new**" story or adventure	Wrote a "**new**" adventure for Joe and his thought-zapping power that was 3 sentences long	Wrote a "**new**" adventure for Joe and his thought-zapping power that was more than 3 sentences long	

Assessment, Lesson 6

Outcome		Criteria			Total
	1 (Not yet)	2 (Meets)	3 (Fully Meets)	4 (Exceeds)	
Students write an adventure about themselves and their thought-zapping power that is 3 or more sentences long	Did not write an adventure about themselves and their thought-zapping power	Wrote a story relating to themselves, but not a include their thought-zapping power	Wrote an adventure about themselves and their thought-zapping power that was 3 or more sentences long	Wrote an adventure about themselves and their thought-zapping power that was more than 3 sentences long	

SOME COLOURING PAGES

Captain: _____

(your name)

Captain Joe Teaching Resources

Captain: _____

(your name)

Captain: _____

(your name)

www.ingramcontent.com/pod-product-compliance
Lightning Source LLC
Chambersburg PA
CBHW080519110426

42742CB00017B/3167